THE TAPESTRY AND THE WEB

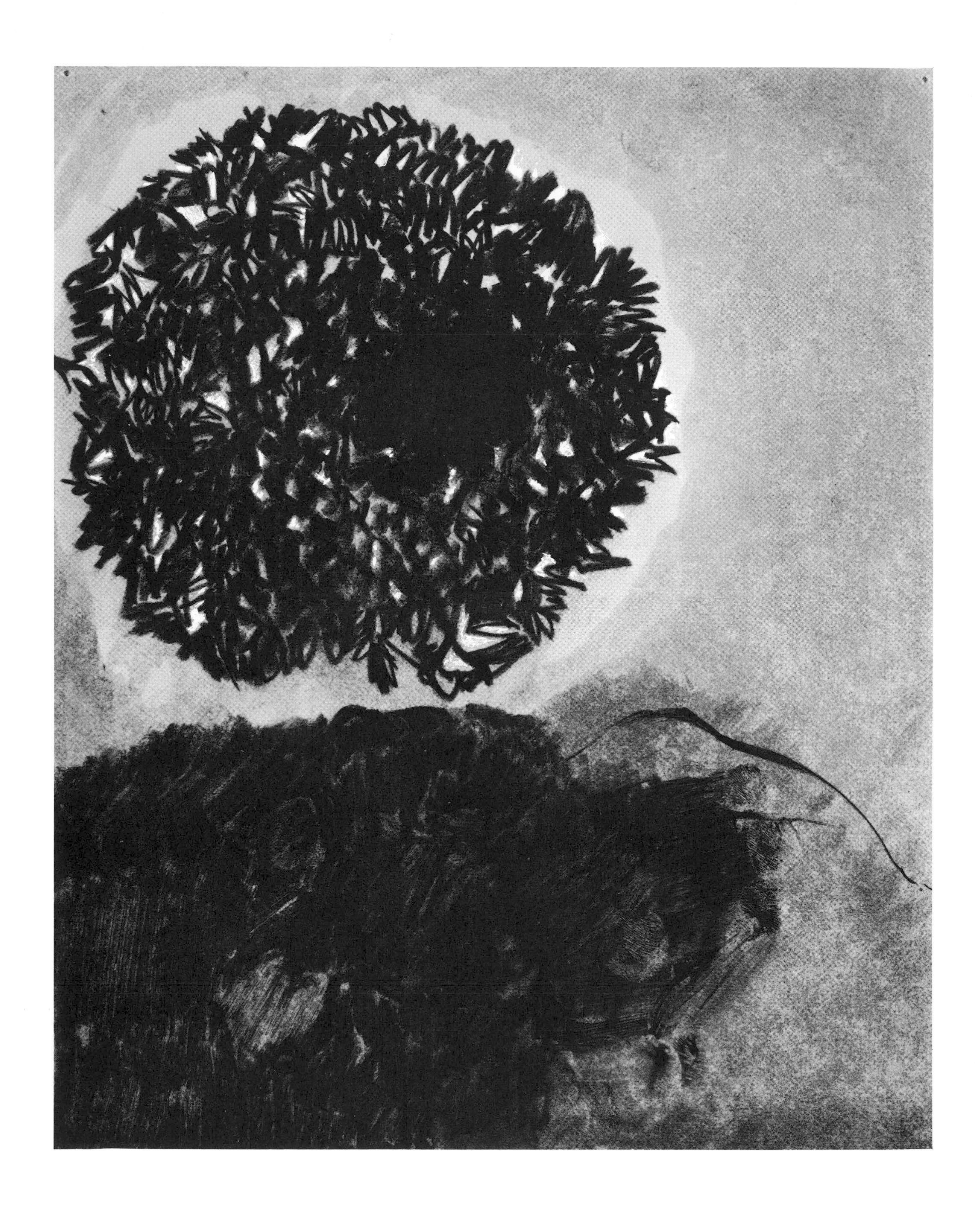

WRITING 5

THE TAPESTRY AND THE WEB

Joanne Kyger

FOUR SEASONS FOUNDATION SAN FRANCISCO : 1965

Published by Four Seasons Foundation
with East Wind Printers

Distributed by City Lights Books, 261 Columbus Ave.
San Francisco, California 94111

Contents

THE TAPESTRY AND THE WEB

THE MAZE

I saw the
dead bird on the sidewalk
his neck uncovered
and prehistoric

At seven in the morning
my hair was bound
against the fish in the air
who begged for the ocean
I longed for their place

Behind the
tall thin muslin of the curtain
we could see his shadow
knocking
and we waited
not stirring
crouched by the fireplace
where the ashes blew out

later we checked the harbor
to see if it was safe
rather hoping
one had gone astray
and flung itself upon the shore
for all to watch

If I should weep
they would never know

and so I walked
silently
shrugging off hands
in treacherous places
wanting to fall

In Williamsburg, Virginia

my uncle
pointed out the Maze
which grew
in the dead
governor's garden

delighted

I went to it

and stood
poised

inside the
precise
entrance

like a long hallway
the tightly trimmed
bushes
held themselves
pointing each
leaf
and twig
in an unquestioning manner

white gravel
caressed my feet

the sky disappeared
and I
could hear
the sound of water
rushing

I knew each corner
without pausing

Held captive in a cave
Ulysses
sobbed for his wife
who was singing high

melodies
from the center of a
cobweb shawl
of their design

three feathers
I picked
from a stone
in my path

and turning at last
I saw
the speckled bench
and halting fountain
which marked
the end.

She

tortures

the curtains of the window

shreds them

like some

insane insect

creates a

demented web

from the thin folds

her possessed fingers

clawing she

thrusts them away with

sharp jabs of long pins

to the walls.

1958

Tapestry

The anticipation of one
grey hound
his front
legs raised

The faces of
five huntsmen
show
the legend

A million leaves
and flowers
placed into
life   they

are urgent.

And to drink I
must bow
down
before you

small birds   they
taste of your life

they
know
they
know
and

quickly

music sounds on my
ear

brush the
green oak and
holly
heron and
peach tree
caught

The mother has
blest us   and I

am surrounded
by the life
not of this
story

6.58

The Long Poem

I desire the
        sleep that lets me move

without my feet
deciding which way
to go

I suffer from the drug

            use what displeases me

                    ghosts and phantoms

                            the love of he who
                            seems a stranger
                            but his eyes they
                            are the same

                            balances on two legs
                            waving front hands foolishly
                            before like paws

                            strange the resemblances

                I arrange my own murder

and lay my head
down on the pillow
purple and stained

Youngster — don't babble
to me I
am tired

We were steering a course close to shore where the
sound of breakers could be heard through the fog.

a reekish stench of
death in the kelp beds.

the wind stops

over us like sleep
it is not pleasant
the sail flaps

— a listless excursion

we wait for movement
incompatible — not hostile
vaguely annoyed with each other
one of us should start to paddle.

I expect Virgil
to guide across the
ripple tops to
guide the prow still
further into the gloom

Where are we caught?
This mist obscures
the landmarks

Sounds seem at hand's distance and
slaps against the broadside lessen

Down I reach but
there is no wetness I
feel my hand
pass on through it searching — dead wing of a gull
urchins
hermits of the ocean floor
jelly monsters
the garbage of the
kelp bed and those
that feed upon it

there
only with my touch.

This is no river
yet my eyes see only
lengths to each side

and the rhythm of those roars

off to my right

to what do they belong?

You turn a
ghost
I cannot speak.

We wait.

. . . .

We wait and
what for I

know that we should paddle to the dock
no wind will come

and then I will take down the jib sail, wash salt from the decks,
this is my job, make sure the mooring knot is tight and
walk through the damp to the car.

.

We drive up
and out
into the sunshine
and see
from this mountain side

the blanket which stops
short
a little after the harbor.

the sea down there
undulating in the fog

But the sun is oppressive
it is too hot.

the sage crackles
and you cannot smoke
for fear
from fire

Sharp light bounces off
the exposed rock face
to one side of us —

an intensity overbearing —
as if in combustion we
will perish,
an explosion of a moment

one dry movement
the lizard

he has been here for three thousand years
I have found him embedded in shale, same
size and shape

blinks a dry lid
glass eye.

once.

remains
clinging
in the sun
on a piece of
corrugated rusted iron.

I turn to walk away but
cannot move my feet

they are not lead
lead would become

molten in this place

Yet so heavy I
fall to my knees

stumps
grown down into the
side of this mountain
surrounded by the
dry and gritty dust

I call to you to
free me but
you have disappeared and

All I see before me is the
hot shine of the
rock face
and the glint
from the lizard's eye.

Must I remain?
The fathers of the Sierras
once crossed here and
went beyond
Steadily made the
trails we came up on
Tracked down with sandaled feet
the yellow dirt of this mountain

I do not see their bones

How did they move
across this sun?

I do not know any of this.

Turning my head it
slips by

then changes about
and coming face to face

tosses me like
a bull   the minoan youth.

Yet I have been so careful . . .

wrapped myself in
laughter and the
clatter of my tongue

but look what has happened

I see the unicorn
before me
prancing
tapping an
impatient golden hoof

How does he know me and
what does he want?

She has turned to a tree
her long arms willow

and what am I?
a flower
a deer
a spider waiting
for the breeze to
speed my weaving

the reverie of

memory past
what I know.

I come to take roses
step into the
precise place of this
circle and fountain

Gather into my arms
flowers of each color
bush to bush

I hear him laughing
in the fountain
mirthful

rises up
the sun is still

the pressure of his hand
upon the top enclosure
stops the water falling

where is the tune to lull the grass
bend iris back that
deer may pass to drink

the sparrow falls to my shoulder

His face he observes
as if unknown
caressed by lips of water

Unreal God
he moves to me

My arms are full of
unused roses
caught by the thorn I weep.

Pursued.

pursued along the dirt path
up to the stable.

Who threw the pebble
    down on the road
    at night where I ran
    not even the moon
    or the sound of animals

Pursued   she
    makes me leave
    through the windows
    through the circle of horses
                wild under the smell of the sycamore
                and the light of the pleiades

                Possessed
                hair as a mane
        gardens, thistles, sweet anise crushed   I run

She makes me run
   splashing thru the
   eroded stream rivulets

            bare feet suck the ground the
            heifer rushes to the barbed wire

Heart pounding
I run   her
eyes on my shoulder

       at the top of the hill
       there are no trees

Waiting, lurking
in the underbrush
           her mouth,
           teeth
           catching the sound of the night

I run   crashing thru the
  corn stalks
  frantic at the bramble thorns that stop me

Sick
I see the house it
has no light   she
steps across the door.

•

I have not come here to die

We wage a war
She has placed on the shelves
honey and dried stuff for the winter
and bound me down to my chair

Yet I have not come here to die
My wrists perform their tasks surely
My hands are obedient
I did not think they would be

I cannot see what she does
they tell me her performance is equal
I do not believe them

She sends messengers: barn swallow
dragonfly
tree squirrel

She sends them to watch: field mouse
opossum
grasshopper

and they stay.
I take nothing from her
every thread is my own,
falls across my feet and
into the corners of the room
there is much to tell

I will not die
her face is turning old
her fingers hesitate
there is skill in my unfolding that frightens her
Who is the prisoner?

I surely will not die
looping sea into flower
beast into stone.

A parallel
unplanned
displays our
names   we

travel through that
climax of a hundred
stories all our
own and
of our making

take unto ourselves
the days of every life
          and do not know it

He moves at ease
  about the room
  touching color to the wall

- they ride as ropers, saddlemen
  clowns in suits of armor

- robust on small donkeys
  spurs — dark shapes against
                unwilling flanks

He propels them — two figures
        four
        how many I cannot count
their stillness only in paint
lines impatient, hovering

    Is it caprice that
makes him capture the beast
and turn him aside
        head askew
        tail lashing

A sureness

dictates the fall of each animal
the real smell of dust
      hung dead by their heels
      what runs down their sides
            but desire from his hands?

Ponderously she drags her belly up the
shore to drop the eggs

he sings of it in a low voice
made husky by the night

she leaves her eggs on the
high sand line
their birth has been done
she will leave them
   wrapped in dune grass

heavily she moves her
legs to the outgoing tide water
her home in the dark of the sea
breeding place

and who will cover them with
   palm branches   the sun
will open the shells
a crawling mass of
open mouths

she has dropped them
the work is finished
this birth a chore
they devour each other

the heedless spawning
a heavy bearing

he drums this beat from the
low thatched roof
crouches low on his heels
he sings of her belly
and the sigh of the ocean

THE DANCE

a step into
the dance
this
progression towards
creation

the Ceylonese Bodhisattva
                        12 centuries old

seated
    one heel out
leans
   thighs bent
as if he will
enter into the dance

an excitement
from the position of his body
we make one movement / repeat it

he is poised as if to make
the new one

wrist bent out
three fingers touch
the palm of this hand
    Body sleek

and wet as if rising from the river

assured
the rising
the step
is his
when he pleases.

What new way to look at stars
the eye
sees
as ever
they are yellow/ I remember

and the grass
the long wet grass
smelling new
wet

and blue-green about the feet
fields of it.

We walk a while
the sky still pale
I am concerned with the echo
it answers perfectly
one does not find
canyons like this

often/ lined with growth
tangles of ivy

Stay with me
Stay with me

like scribe in
grecian robe I

draw in dust the
revolutions of the sky

the balance of the universe is
planned by formula

Aristotle tells us
the deductions are not mine —
observe

the jealous suitors are
driven by no logic

they pay homage
at night
group themselves
and fall
breaking the orderly progressions

the interjections of their voice
come near us

their whispers heard/ it
drives us
— we pace top portions of the earth
and will not partake of their food.

. . .

For how long we sit
in quiet

absurd this way no
speech
creates a
tie between us

the bobbing atoms of Democritus/ he
knew the interruptions of the air
contain our destinies

This tongue denies the touch/ I
tell you so/ but this one way to
keep you here is

all I have discovered

for I am young and
young no longer

that rose of Dante's will not bloom
across the landscape here

and though I try to start again
the offering is limited

the size of my hand cupped/ is
small to drink from

such entertainment
without diversion
I forget the feel of skin

Repeat and
repeat again
over
the long cry of the
bird at night

What new way to
change its song.

Summer and fall 1958

Tapestry

the eye

is drawn

to the Bold

DESIGN —— the

.Border.

.California flowers.

nothing promised that isn't shown.

Implements:

shell
stone

.Peacock.

Somewhere you can find reference to the fact that PAN was the son of PENELOPE

Either as the result of a *god*

or as a result of ALL of the suitors

who hung around while Odysseus was abroad.

We are in a tighter web than I had imagined.
that story
about him capturing a girl in the woods was a lie!
The rest of the commentators too
are shocked at its impiety

Bred of the weaver it's his
Looks that do it.
rather bold.
All the result of impatience & he
is impatient himself a
restless eye.
but solid.
sticking close to what he knows
pretty well.

My mother always remembered the
crippled boy in her grade school class room who teased her.

he was ugly.
of another sort.

But then are You one
or many. Could I meet you, drive away the
children who beat you with sticks.

But then I forget you
have been made by that excellent craftsman, she
is lovely.

That is why they depend on you. Each one
demands you. And the flowers. I
trust those flowers although I admit now damnit
that I never knew their names.

can I reconcile you with nasturtium

I've got to move
very carefully now.
.there was a meadow flower from the mountains which was promised me
and never brought.

But I am here now
only the spoken name is different now

11.59

12.29 & 30 (Pan as the son of Penelope)

Refresh my thoughts of Penelope again.

Just HOW
solitary was her wait?

I notice Someone got to her that

barrel chested he-goat prancing
around w/ his reed pipes

is no fantasy of small talk.
More the result of BIG talk
and the absence of her husband.

And what a cockeyed lecherous offspring. What a birth
THAT must have been. Did she turn away & sigh?

I believe she dreamed too much. Falling into her weaving,

creating herself as a fold in her tapestry.

a flat dimension character of beauty
keeping one task in mind and letting nothing *Human* touch her
— which is pretend.

She knew what she was doing.

OUTSIDE
of that he grabbed her.

Some thing keeps escaping me. Something

about the landing of the husband's boat upon the shore.

She did not run up and embrace him as I recall.

He came upon her at the house & killed the suitors.

I choose to think of her waiting for him
concocting his adventures bringing
the misfortunes to him
— she must have had her hands full.

And where did she hide her impudent monster?

He was acres away by then I suppose in the sunlight leching
at some round breasted sheep

girl.

the cock crowing at dawn never had bigger thoughts than he did

about waking up the world.

A song in the rope   taut against the wind
A song in the wire   taut against the wind

Needless to say this could have been his very course
He *did*
travel far away
from where she waited

But bitches there are
even at sea — although that one takes a bit more
tender handling, it's still all bluff
a matter of riding out the storm.

Now wind is another matter
that is who he had to close his ears to

and worse at night the sound, I am You, I am You, Join.

and what does it touch which is deep
and are men willingly driven over rails

a scream higher than a woman's
at any forbidden place.

. .

I am watching what is happening now
it seems that water is being pushed from both sides of the boat
as we make our passage thru it.
We don't have to stop

and can hardly blame our follies to the breeze.

waiting again
what for

I am no picker from the sea of its riches
I watch the weaving — the woman who sits at her loom
What was her name?   the goddess I mean
— not that mortal one

plucking threads
as if they were strings of a harp

Spring, 1960

They are constructing a craft
solely of wood
at Waka-no-ura, fishing village,
a jewel quite naturally
from the blue of the farm house tile roofs.

found on the southern coast.

The women pull by hand long strings
of seaweed across the shore
it dries
At the other end of the town
the hull of the boat rises
above the smaller houses
A little prince of a boy in a white knit suit
stands with the others in a group on the beach

Watching us go by, we are strange.

The women bend over
the seaweed, wakame, changing its face to the sun.

It is lonely

I must draw water from the well   75 buckets for the bath

I mix a drink — gin, fizz water, lemon juice, a spoonful
of strawberry jam

And place it in a champagne glass — it is hard work
to make the bath

And my winter clothes are dusty and should be put away

In storage.   Have I lost all values I wonder
the world is slippery to hold on to

When you begin to deny it.

Outside outside are the crickets and frogs in the rice fields

Large black butterflies like birds.

vision of heaven & hell

11.3.61

only hells so far.
where the floor slanted
down the hall
the street light during the day
also dipped in the street
100 deaths in the newspaper murder
on every page in the back seat
of the greyhound bus to Stinson Beach.

hours in advance
things entering the door a second time
from the corner of my eye a dark
wild pig, he had long thin legs.

This goes all around again

where heaven explodes the walls.
against the pattern of fleur-de
-lis and bulls, flowers, ladies sewing
marigolds
all part of doom — that's hell, all of the fantasy men
and women
underground

the ceiling of earth where hell pushes up
they are flowers
and spider webs. minstrels with lute stories

spun out, *connected*
and put together
And seasons spring
and fall, our knowledge, expectancy.
he said the same thing again
and remembered, it is creation that remains,
is hell.

outside where the storm goes cracked
he says you cant come in
hold the baby under your saree
and I'm going to sit up here and watch you
in this purple velvet lined tower of
mine, and look at the fruit tree
and watch all the red and yellow pears and
cheeries jiggle when it lightnings and
after while maybe I'll have
the chokidar bring up some tea and a plum
and a whole bunch of candy and stuff
and you'd just better stay down there
and get all crummy and muddy.

Caption for a miniature

1962

My Sister Evelyne

Sarnath
Tuesday, February 13
near the evening, 5:05

the child with his temper tantrum
this morning on the deer park path
his white satin dress
rolling
on the red ground.   Evelyne
every morning in Illinois
screeching
on the kitchen floor
before breakfast exhausting
us all, she also cried
when we gave her a new rubber doll
in despair
her glasses fastened around her head
with a wide rubber band
black eyes crossed
in rage.
all of us waiting for gratitude

She had a plaid dress
that we took her to school in. She was sent home
too young. In her harness and green snow
suit straining, pink cheeks
chapped. The father
stands holding her back from the snow.

At 8 she sat in the carved high backed
chinese chair
quietly, Nancy thought she was ill
at my 14th birthday party

Louise is her middle name
a foul tongued determination
brought material rewards for her
an extra piece of meat, TV dinners served
in the dark, expensive shoes.
perfect teeth

Tapestry

Dealing with the detail
on the fragment of the fifth
Tapestry the maid whose head
is turned sideways her eyes
shifted upwards in what
seems
coquettish towards
the sound of the
huntsman's horn the
capture
then of the
unicorn. Her hair is uncombed.
and hand
raised up in a lackadaisical gesture
meaning all's well.

You can tell.
Puffeyes and the broken turned nose.
Searching
for bigger & better things.

4.62

Burning the Baby to make him realer

Dipping him at night in the kitchen
the rest are asleep
by one hand into the flames
just out of a desire of niceness
The lady of the earth wandering
in sorrow
tries to give him a gift but he screams
& the mother awakes rushing into the room

And where is my daughter, where is she
I'll teach you all a lesson
you'll never forget

Gary says of the blond child
tensely crouching on the porch he's
not human.   at 2½ an unfaltering
icy blue stare in his eyes he DEMANDS
Both hands before him, uh-uh,
want, want
& his parents cower
what is it, what is it you want.
a wake of smashed cookies, crushed lipstick wet cigarettes
& nervous haste, no joy
ripping the morning glories 3 times from the pot

Iliad: Achilles does not die

Leaving him alive abruptly that way
& the burial & the keening
for the other at the end of the dry plain
the stream burned alive
the wave crashing down dies
mid-way

12 men sacrificed for Patrocles

. .

How big was the distance of Troy
& the battlefield, the shoreline
of ships — does it stretch as far
as the city of Kyoto

. . .

& no more of Helen
who takes her back? soft as
a throw of silk
& she said, perhaps
I dreamed it all.

. . .

the length & breadth
of all that chasing

. .

& Helen still quiet at home
tending to the needs of the household —

how Homer dislikes Paris

& here is Achilles stript stript left.
waits, but the story ends
this blanket of air
& the tenderness of mortals.

fragmented. ie

several valleys.

Unfortunately unable to give you the plain *D.* can present of
wheat, corn etc. only bravado on my part
to hope to be blessed with complete vision. I'm sure
you can see me better
than I can.
Dealing with one sided particulars, loneliness
contempt & godliness,
Play is occasional
scrambling around by accident.

. . .

We took the left fork
up into Yase valley at the rise of the hill, used only
by woodsmen, charcoal makers.
moving farther
and farther back into the valley burning trees as they go
Situated on near inaccessible
hillsides and their families, smoking out the wood.
Way up on top
where you'd like to think he was a poet hermit
grunting in the cold, fixing up his charcoal,
not reveling
in any city way about nature
maybe he's mean. all their abandoned junk
from house to house.
The greased log rails
for pulling lumber,
12 inches apart or so, on my hands and knees.

. . .

packing all the lacquer boxes
with mild tasting flavors, off to Ninaji
cutting off the new back highway
with yellow dirt exposed like the west
& the last of the 200 shrines all dusty now & the windows torn
for the famous double nosed cherries.

5,000 cups of sake later
talent abounds & the leaves pulled off the tree.

.

She dances
She dances
gravely.

this way
& that, an arm
or a fan
for her face, and her feet
hardly turn

. . .

Picking up & using
everything, the gravel
on the river bed
and the river moves on
that's what it is.
and the water changes too, hardly the same drop
gets through. that's all we can hope for

2.63

Look the bird is making plans
talking to men in the room upstairs
poking at crumbs in the kitchen
using *our* toilet
& whose rights do I worry about
Keep the house
I'll
go bird you keep this place
at the very farthest wall
pushing & scratching to get out
thru the cracks in the batten
where the light comes in after storms
& the weeds tear thru in August
all all
has fled
has gone flicked by
& scratched the soil.
& you claw foot   fix it
fix it   I'm going.

4.63

The Hunt in the Wood: Paolo Uccello

The greyhounds go leaping into the woods
　　　the hunters behind them
and the trees have their lower branches cut
　　　　So the men with their poles will not be struck
　　　　　and a horse has suddenly stopped
　　　　　on a ring of flowers the rider crying Ho
　　　　　　　　　up to the sky
　　　Small figures way
back in the woods with the hounds shout
　　　The white hounds this way and that
　　like bounding deer or rabbits
　　　　　　　And the deer
here he is with the antlers,　by the pond
　　　　　　　closed in upon
　　They move from the dark of the wood
to the midst, the racing men and their ribbons
　　and the deer rushes back towards them.

My father died this spring
Well, I had meant to write more often
To a kind of hell it must be, with all unresolved difficulties.
I had greens with vinegar last night—that's something
in common
And I would have told him that — adding it
to a list of possible conversations
With the pictures on his dressing table
of all his daughters
but he wasn't flinging out his arms to keep a soul there.
You can't say he wasn't strange
and difficult.
How far does one go
to help a parent like a child — when he waits
at the employees entrance in old clothes
and I don't want him.
Well he'll be there waiting
for me. Demands just, wanted, or not
are to be met.
And let me see, yes the demon large
impossible and yields without vanishing
no power, no satisfaction
sitting on the back porch drinking beer
following me to the sick squirrels in the cellar.
And the material things, calling cards
engraved watches, trunks that married life brings
full of stuff
he left behind 10 years ago. The golf clubs. The fact is
there was a man, a married man,
and an old man. it's impossible to know.
but blood does bring curiosity.

9.15.63

Waiting

over the lilacs won't he   come home

to at least rest tonight,   I want to see

the round car safe in the driveway, cinders

and the moon over head

Those things we see are images of the past

From now, always, on the turning point, viewing back
and that delicious interpretation
is the world, HOW CLEVER OF US

An entirely new thing each time
blind or not about it, always inventive — seeing
stones,
persimmons,
moving a stone in dirt, oh where does it go
she's fleet footed
to be a tree, to be Jack Spicer in a dream
to carry this around all day. and every night
the waves chuck full of things to happen

As clear as you can See
it's done, isn't it, isn't that a *fact.*

Right to the water's edge
That's a wall.
Do you talk to each other well?

I miss each time. up she went her arms went into willow
And do *you* feel
what you put down is fine, precious.

The persimmons are falling
early and rotten from the tree.
no time to attend the garden.
where I go like a dandy
is to the living room
and right to the heart of the matter.

. .

From here to here.
how much are you going to do.
It occurred to me yesterday
people don't die at thirty.
But the bloom is gone. all this
awareness of a bloom to die. what a sad time
when the point is clear and we settle down like ripe wheat
the beginning business over.

. .

There reoccurs a dream
of a large mysterious house, of women in turbans
gigantic attics of rubbish
a long staircase, mysterious inhabitors
of closed off suites, marble fountains,
sneaking through the house
in by the back way, I can't take over.

The great house has strange furniture I'm unfamiliar with.
In a chair in the living room
I don't know a thing, about what's around the corner.
going up the staircase, knocking on the doors.

. .

The different preoccupations. years and years
go by. A bad crop of persimmons eaten with bugs
this year, a good one last. And the wrinkles.
Melting into the nice earth
giving over life, giving it another child.

.

'You've built this vast house, now explore it.'
— Some people have well lived rooms.

December 1963

It always begins I can't
and the ghosts come
hidden refuse in the attic, junk along streams
nothing clear
between objects, fitting, they should sing

Taking the masks of 2 old women hobbling
across the meadow in the dawn, great shapes of trees in the green mist
I can barely see them
and the cold couples entwined
are statues, the grass is so wet
the high old steps, they are 1,000
Look at my face. Sometimes like holding narcissus
everything is good
and fragile as spring, a beautiful thing cupped, the male is the iris
nodding in the sunshine
the great stone statues
rise coupled in a great field sparkling.

I

April 8. The Plan

'Where ever you go I am with you.'
and bring you back.

The morning venus
sailing into the bay,
lifting him asleep onto the land
he has returned to
and doesn't know where he is.
outside of San Francisco
the long paths and eucalyptus
are another country

Oh he is a liar
from the bottom of his heart
But he puts facts together
and has, little rival, and lets no one know.

. .

The real earth
moves and falls away into pieces in the north.
He comes back, was he led astray, the land has abundance
corn and wine, rain
springs , the forest

wild fields of flowers take him out
with your own eyes you make sure

---

there are disguises

the way he dresses
in old clothes and moves like an old man
no one knows the real facts
all the goods he carries and where

can he put them, stow it away, his property
taking it into the mountains
leaving the fine things at home
going into the house
where everything is put in place, set into movement

Oh I have
set eyes on you again, that I should —

the gold, the perfect copper and fine cloth

and set it apart just like stone
2 guarding the entrance to Ithaca

II

Whether he is dead or not and that animal moves up the hall
I am mortal.

The old man, the pig herder, who
like Andy says, tell me what it is,
let me take care of you
The swineherd in charge of the pigs
his oak stockade
made from the heart of the tree
three hundred and sixty
of them to herd.
'I never go to town except for news.
keeping the dogs off strangers. 'See I know
you are hogs
watching the others back in the grove, moving them
They are feeding on acorns they love and drinking water.

. .

'When I returned a second time here there was an evening sun
and I swam ashore
and crouched in the thickets

offered a fine meal.
Take away part of this animal, the ridge of hair, throw it in the fire
and the throat is slit, singe the bristles, cut it up.

She is
goddess of the dawn, her vehicle, the wild boar, stands on him
as a handsome animal.

It moves
outside it is being done
the brightest of all stars

and w/ bristles raised the hogs can run
thru the grove, the ground swept bare, like a kitchen floor would be

He wraps his cloak

and goes out

to watch those pigs

under a rock from the wind.

4.9.64

III

Land at the first point you meet

He wonders whether he will be caught or get through alive
and in the morning tells them all he's leaving.
I see this star up there, thru the white sides of the house, the night is over.

Helen rises

He is given a fine meal to start on his journey
the fire is laid, wood split, meat roasted

and Helen gives him a great robe, embroidered by herself.

At sea bodies are thrown over
seals and porpoise follow the boat. Birds day after day that never rest picking up garbage.

See there is an eagle that ate a goose

He leaves the ship, walking at a good pace

directly to the house of his friend.

4.15.64

April 23. Possibilities
IV

Still after 15 years or more she doesn't know
and may go off with the likeliest and most generous suitor

The best of the lot comes from the corn and grass lands,
wise, and she gives him approval
But what's on her mind?

She never refuses or accepts
stands against a pillar of the house,
watching and planning.

Well the men,
they give a lot of insults to anyone that comes by,
wine running,
dancing with the maids, 112 people
eating every day

She comes and rages
quit eating the coffee cake and cottage cheese
put the lid on the peanut butter jar
sandwiches made of cucumber, stop eating the *food*!

climbing over the rough ravine
and up an impossible cliff, naked, you mark how high you can go
coming back to his opinion of her or hers of him
listening sometimes
to *him* raging, you leave me alone. you dream of me.
and there, she withdrew

and wept for odysseus
until, what bird is it? that swoops in definite circles in the sky
comes down and puts her to sleep

V

Meeting **May 20.**

'for by day my one relief is to weep and sigh

Am I to stay

winding and coming back, goes out and sees, dreams

are awkward things

a cigarette falls behind the bed

I *can't* get out of bed

she pushes

where where are the walls,

out the window the poetry, dishes broken, things torn up, please

please don't weep anymore.

the suitors are sickened w/ blood, look

how they decay, kill them all

an eagle takes a terrified dove

and she places a good chair to hear what goes on

VI

Here it is, the last day. and what has happened.
Penelope had at least one night with her husband.
And he'll have to go on again to find another city

without salt and away from the sea.
She takes this as a matter of course. It is interesting to note

how cautious she was, he called her iron hearted, to see if it was really
he that had returned

until she went to bed. It's good to be clear about what you do.
They had a party. The pigman and cowherd, also the son
drank wine and danced. This was after the killing.
Not a new marriage as some might have thought
12 ladies were hung by the neck.
as usual Penelope slept through all this.

I think she is happy now.
her household is restored.
and she knows he will die an old and comfortable death.
up to your room now to wait a while he tells her
and she does what he says.
I guess it's good to know where you're going.

May 22, 1964

there is no meeting

and they could not string the bow

Memory has no direction,

a soft weeping like rain drumming dry soil

give me a pile of grape leaves

give me a lot of wine

In July

Geraniums

Taking a walk in the morning
the warm mist like rain

Jack picked a nasturtium about 7

Quiet lake with water lilies
no one harms anything that comes down there

the family comes with smiles
thru the large luxurious rooms of the house
scattered thru in white clothing like flowers
take your time, take your time

this is a guest house where all are taken care of
the great and good sun comes out, the sun is a star

She finished up the web, it had to do with her father she said
using it to keep them away for many years, tricking them.
Hermes came to get the dead suitors.
Persephone really died every year
to go down there was difficult a large dark house
and ghost groves on either side one of white. They called her terrible

It has been difficult to write this. One day
I walked around the block, it was grey, and whatever was green on the lawns was clear
the flower pots on the back porch, the neighbor's steps to the second floor
I could have watched for a long time,

why they must go to war I can't decide

to settle fear. we were all born
They are coming towards the house someone calls to Odysseus
and he is that great fighter
having a guide, a female presence who pulls her own self into battle also
A great struggle in Persephone's field of poppies
a broken sprig of geranium
It is not for me to control she calls
the loud men rising towards each other, great turmoils that pull
through all of you, I give you style in battle
the final control is man
Zeus calls halt.
takes all this nature from running riot, the thundering push
of green buds, leaves, grass, roaring
in the sky filling it with birds, the clouds
closing down, mountains rocking, sinks

a flaming bolt, the control takes peace

over an ordered landscape, it is clear
all confusion gone, and nodding their heads wondered where they had gone.

12.1.64

This edition is limited to 1,000 copies
of which 27 are numbered and signed by the
author and specially bound

This book, set in Garamond type,
was designed by Peter Bailey